This Book Is The Property Of

_____

_____

Enhancing The Experience

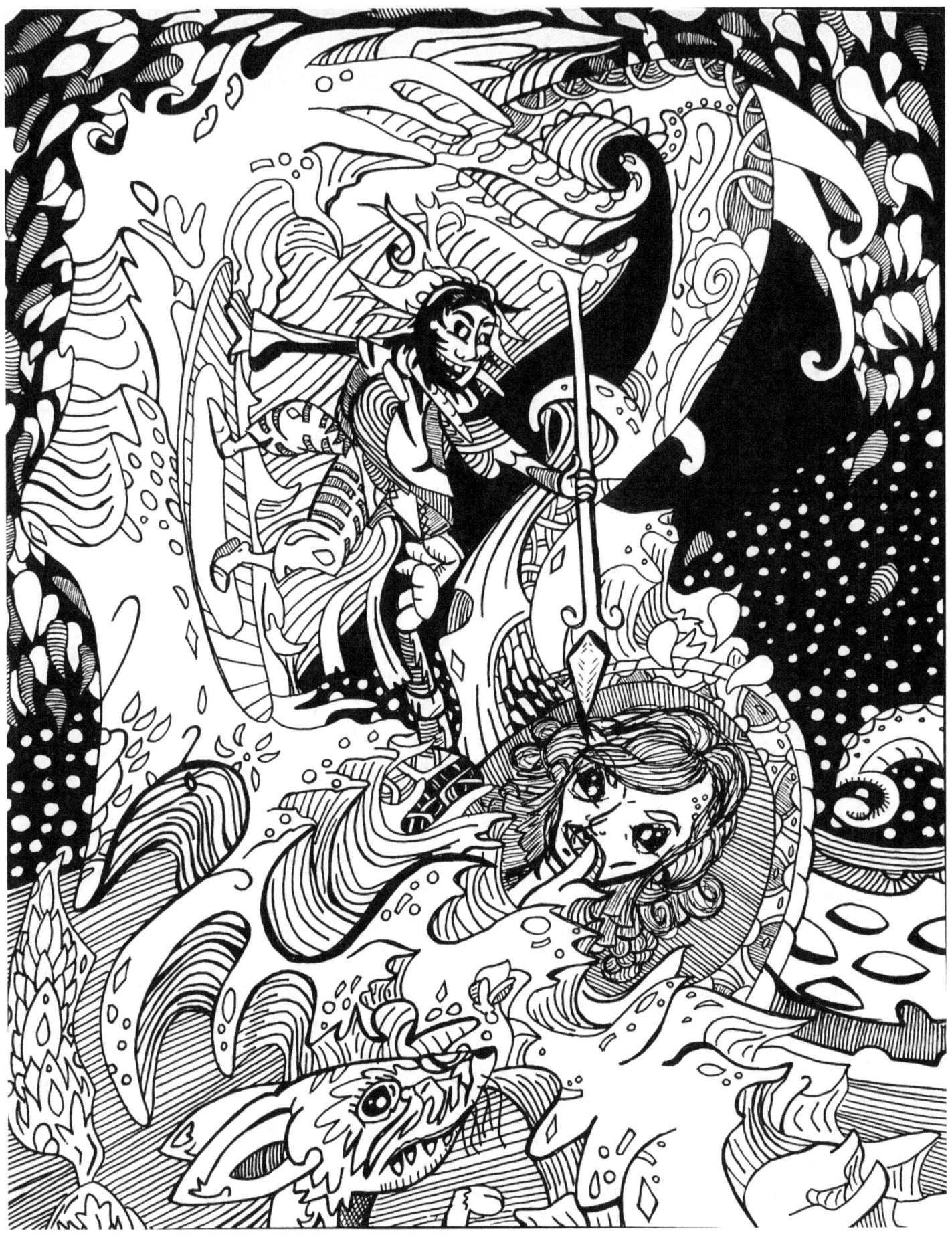

A Dark Fantasy For A Gothic Home

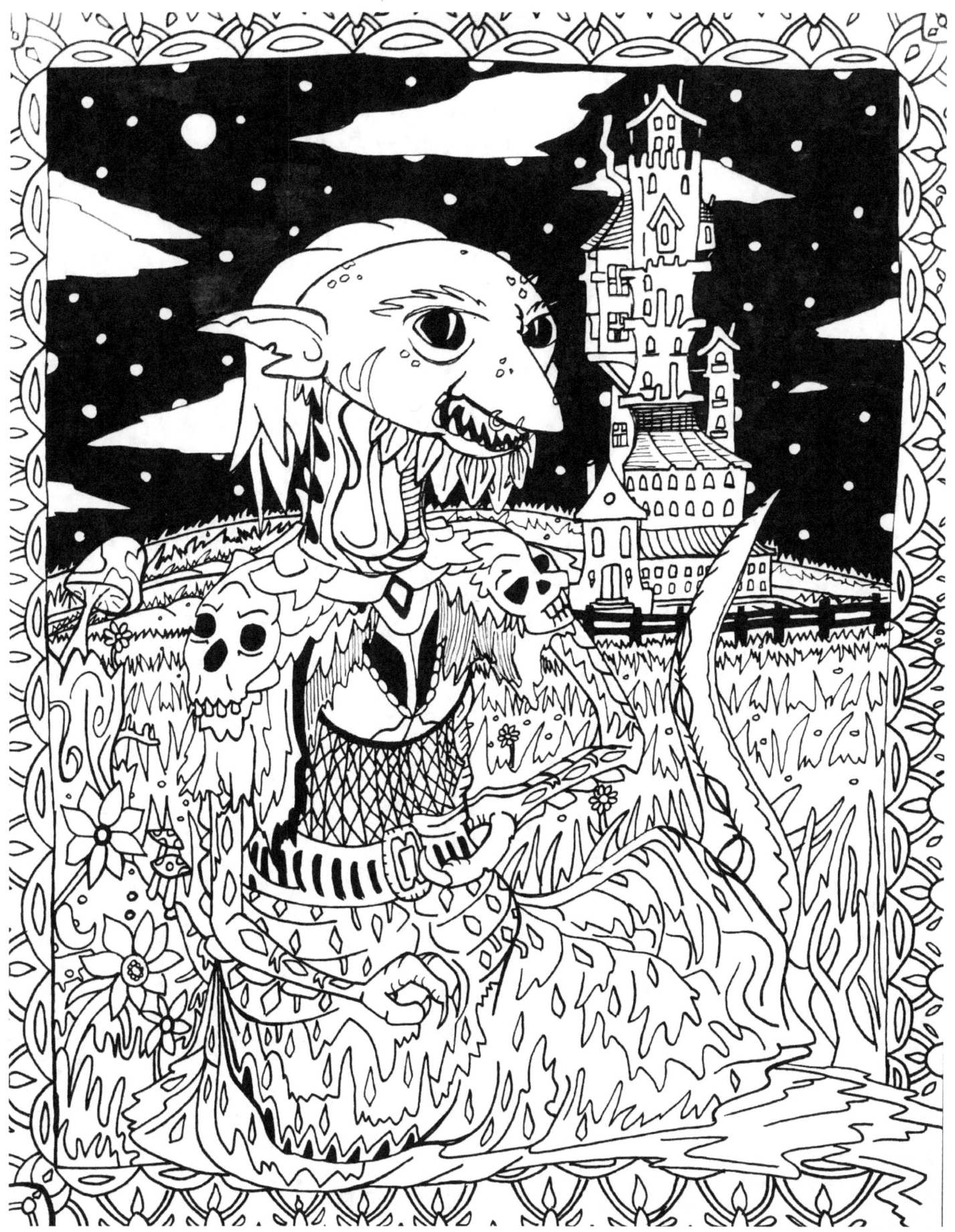

The Relaxation Of Night Magic

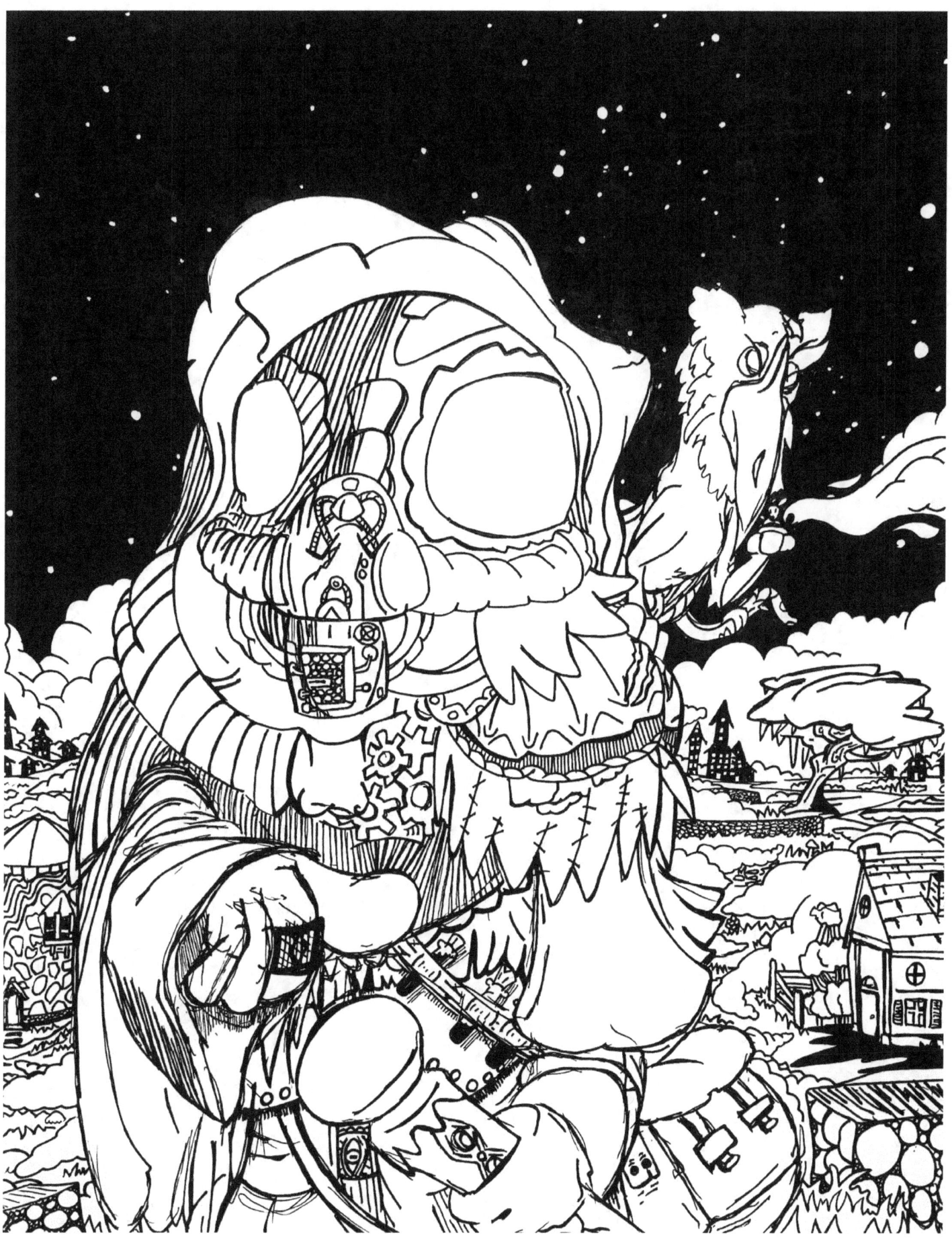

Mythical Chanting

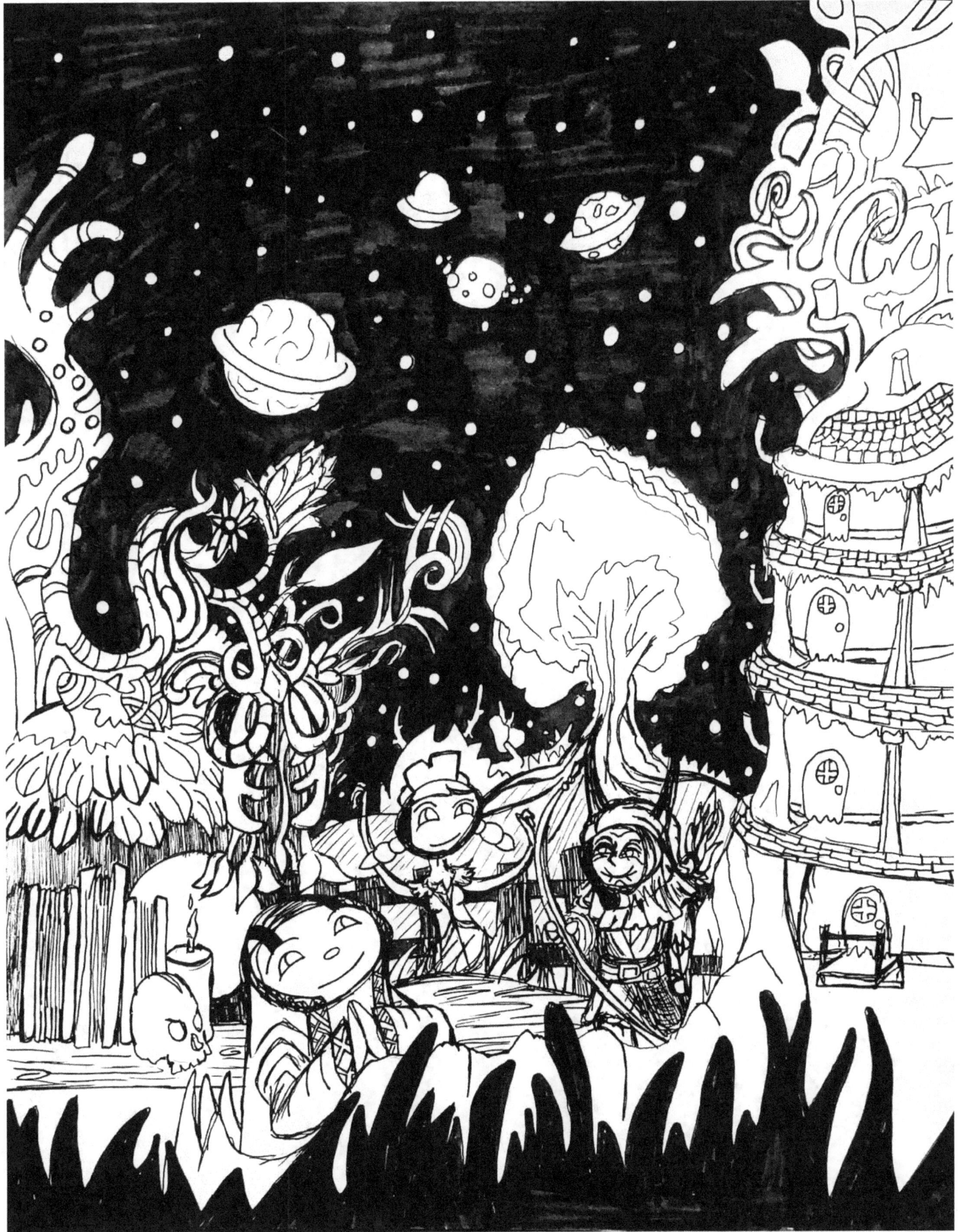

Reveal Yourself

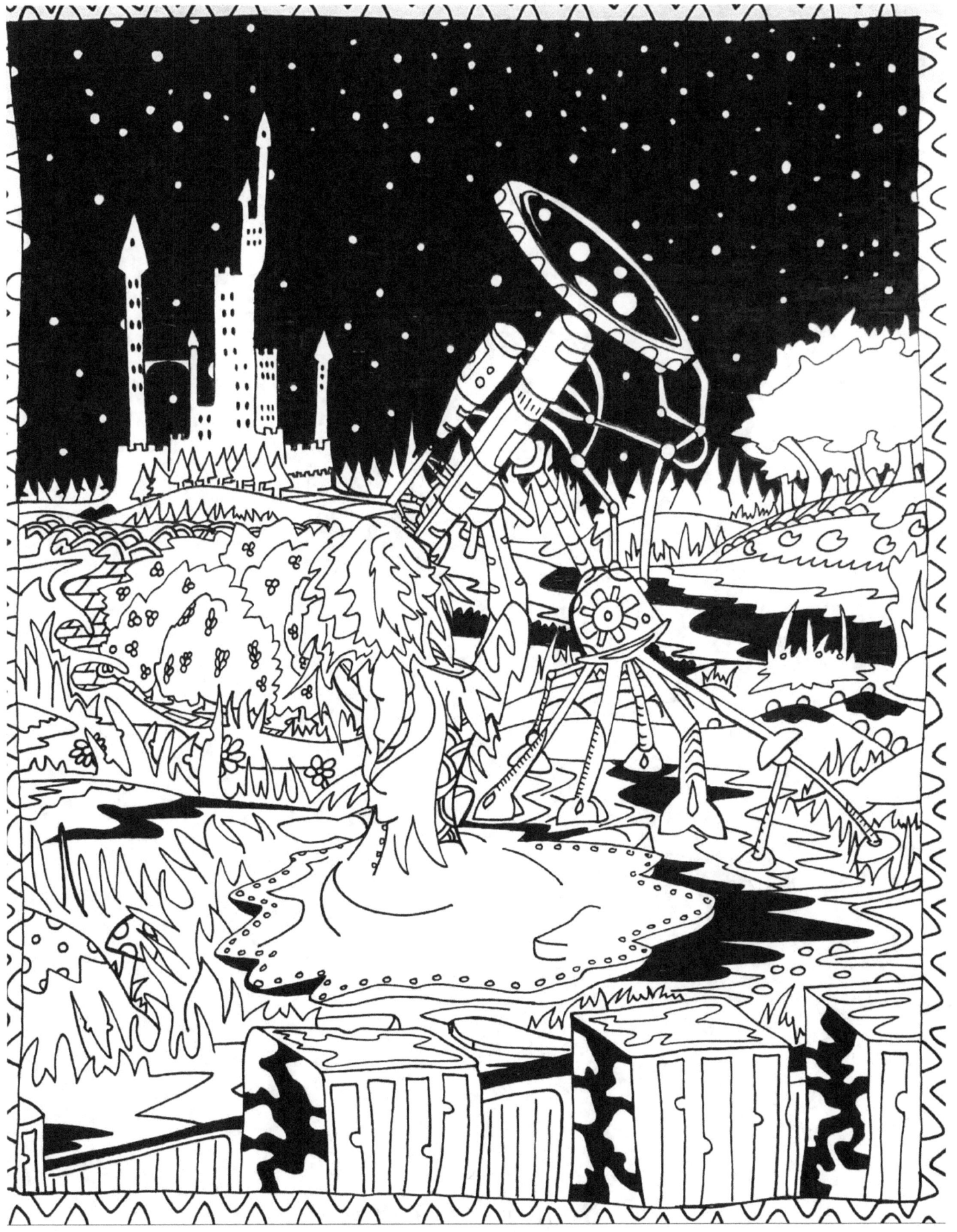

Demonic Mother

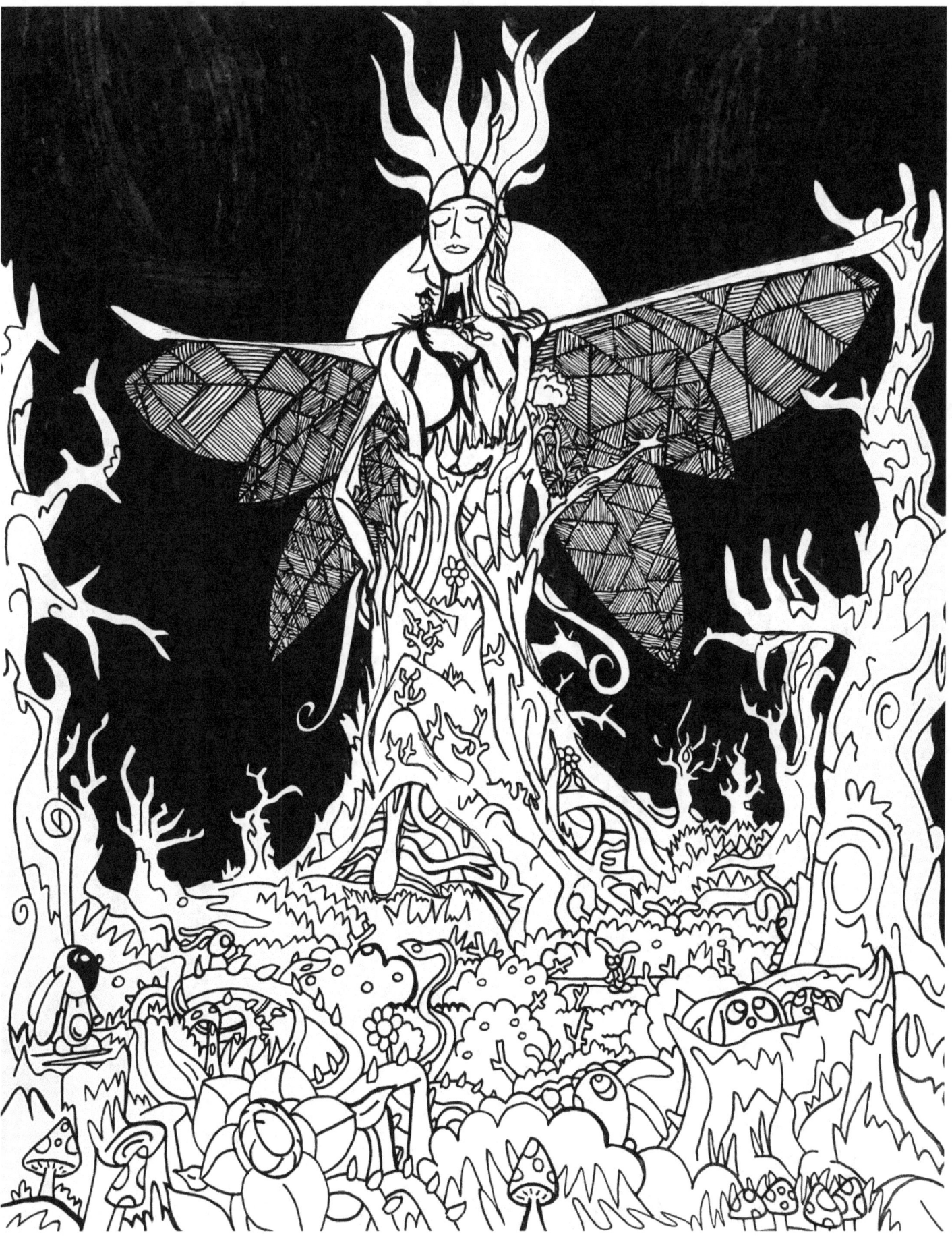

A Dance And Summoning

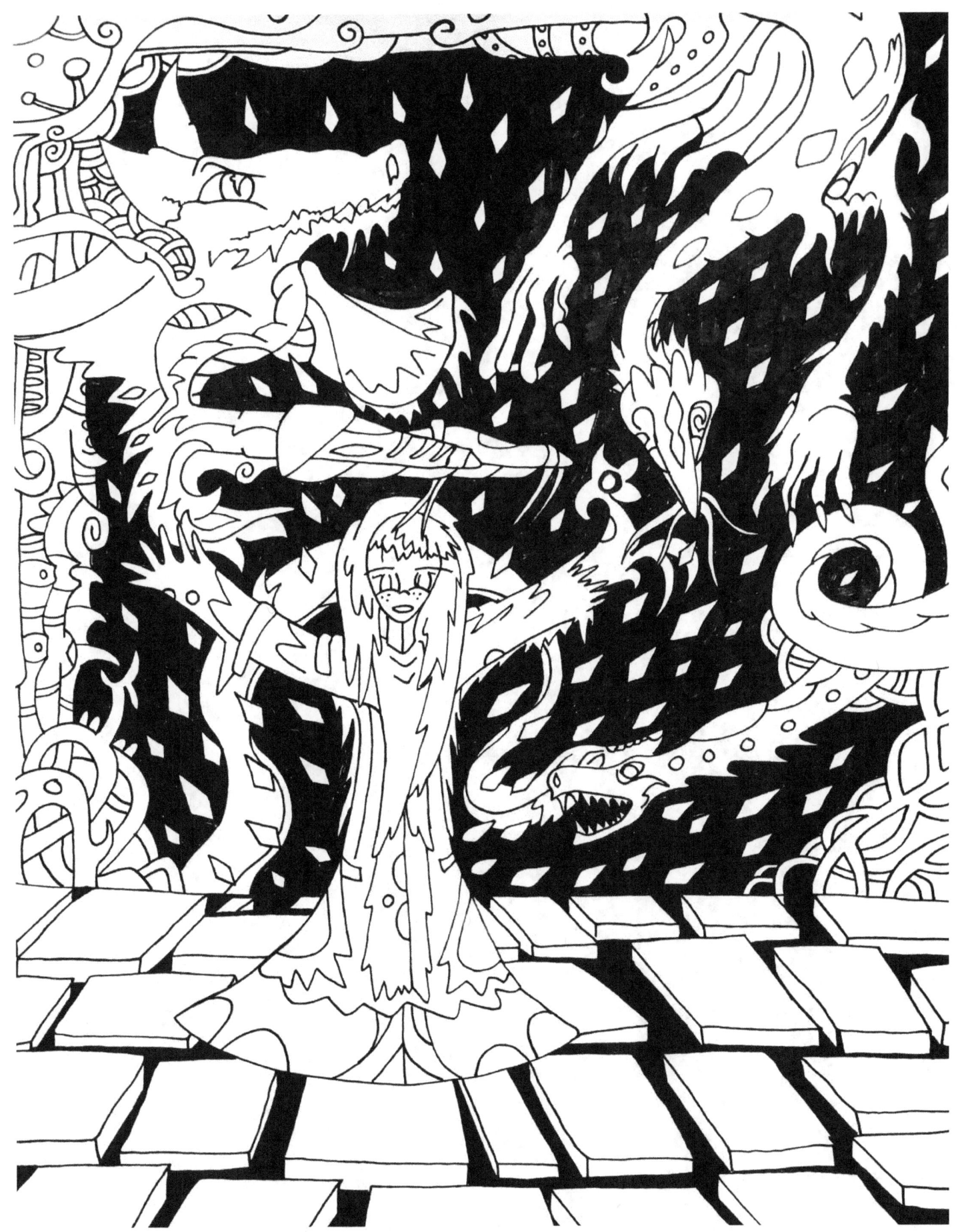

We Were Once Brothers

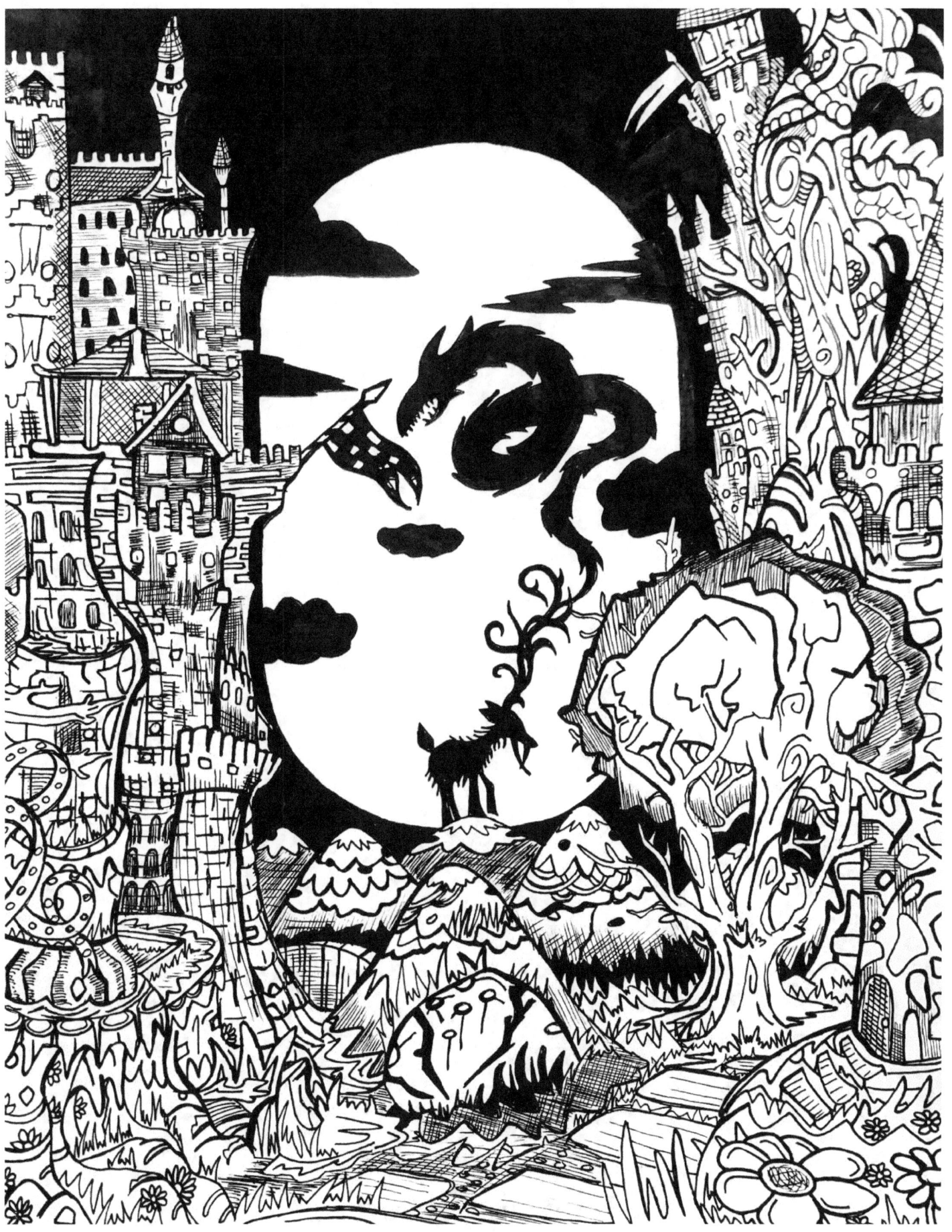

Venomous Beauty

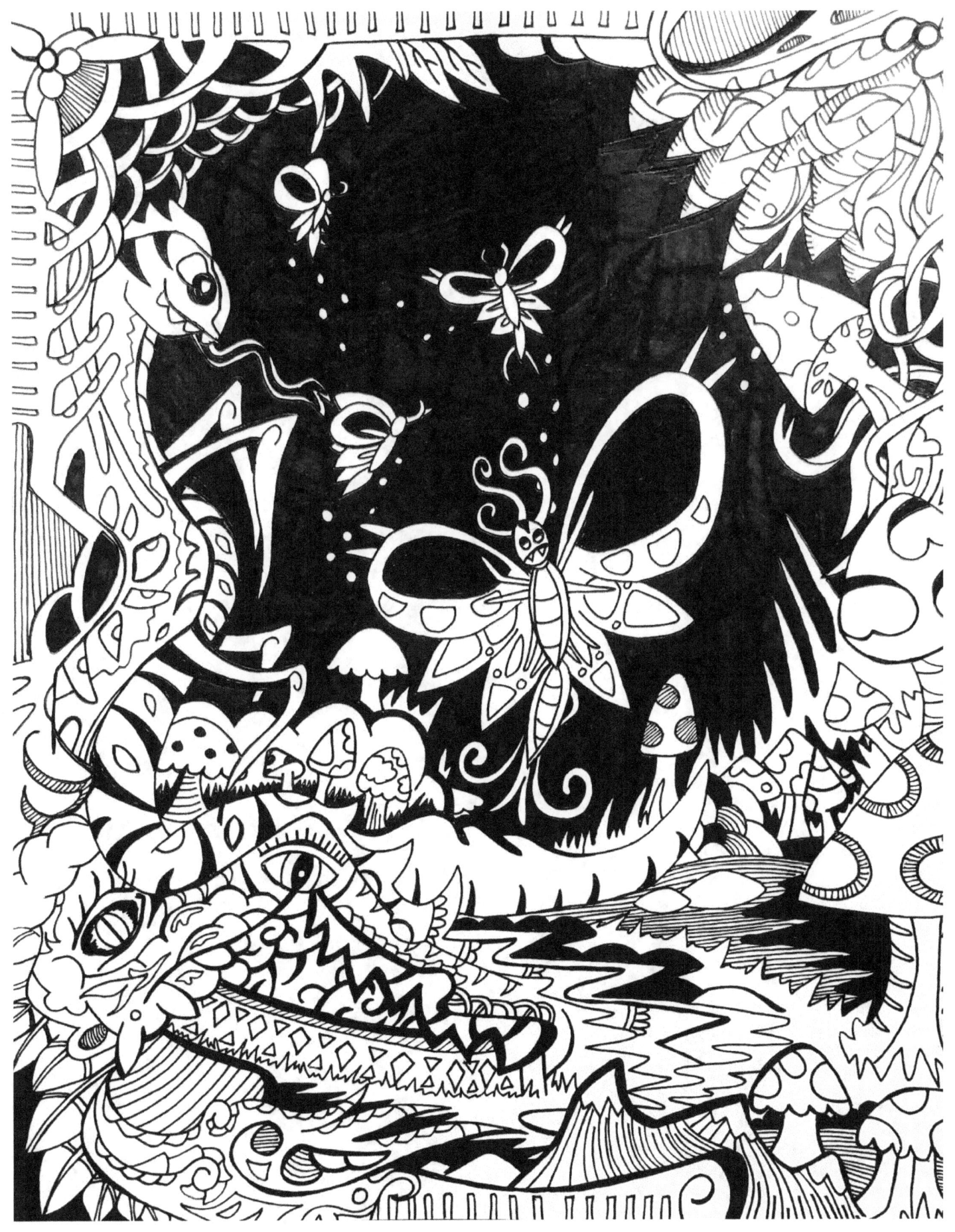

A Lonely Offering

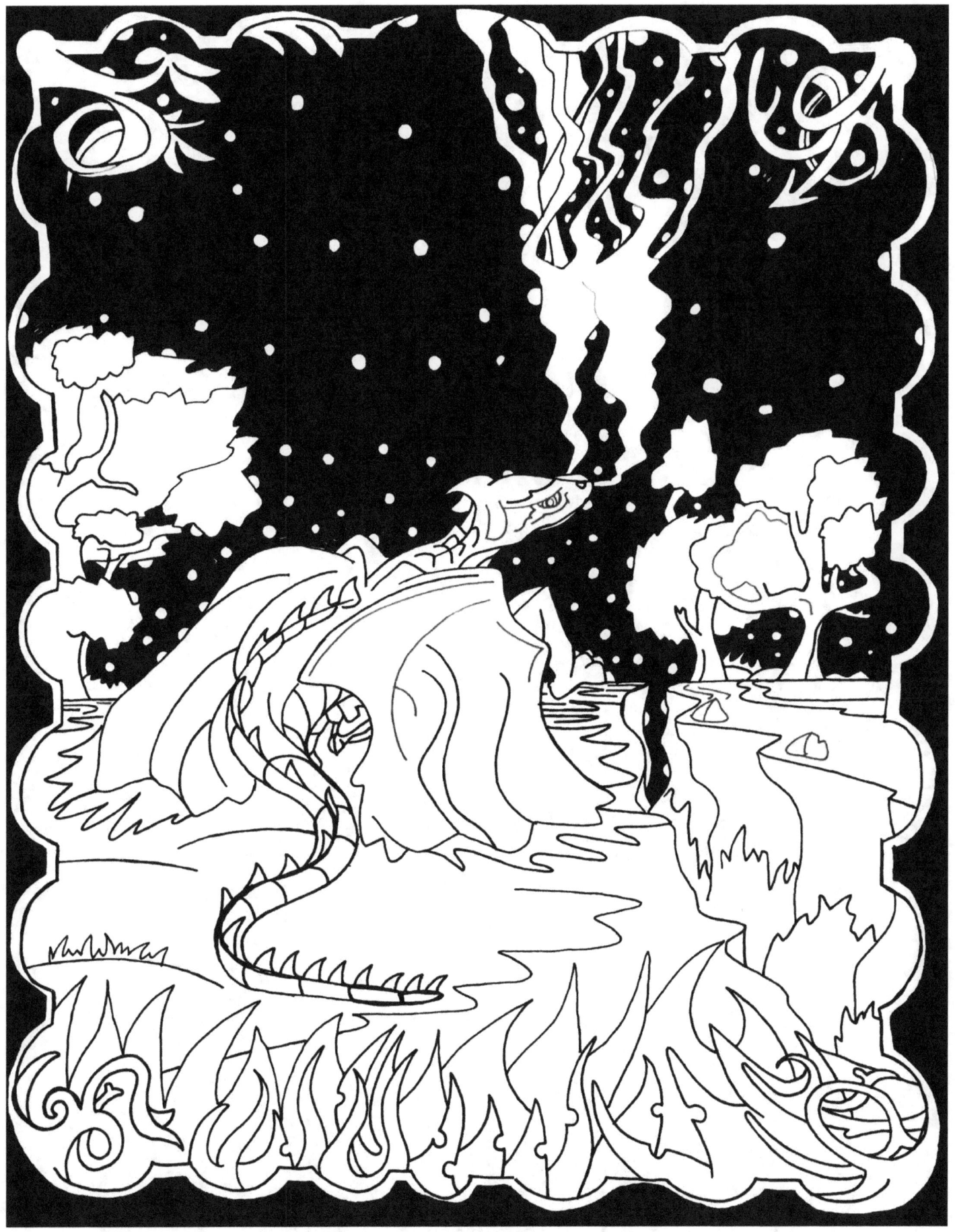

The Shadow Of Those Before Our Altar

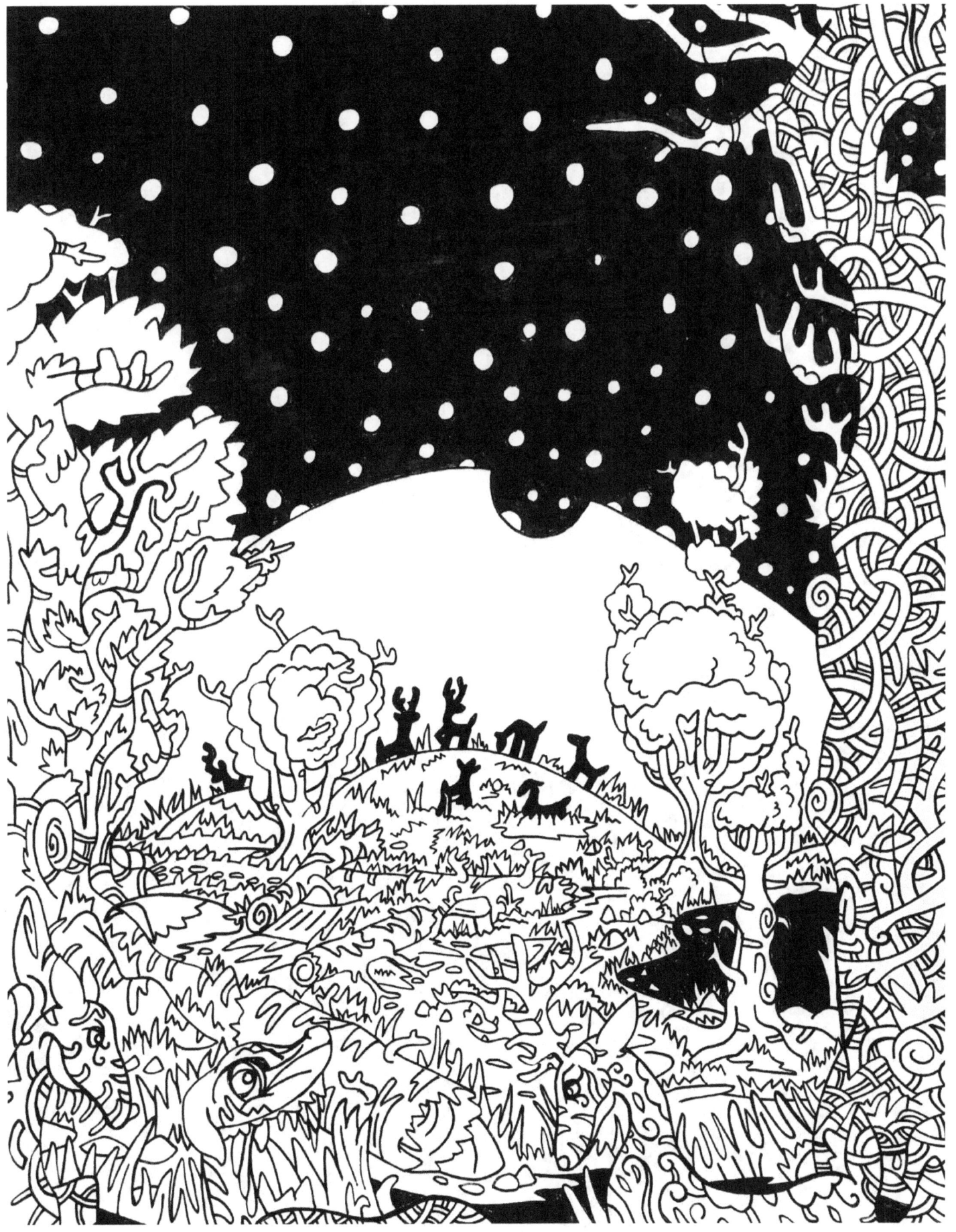

Our Roots Are Seeded

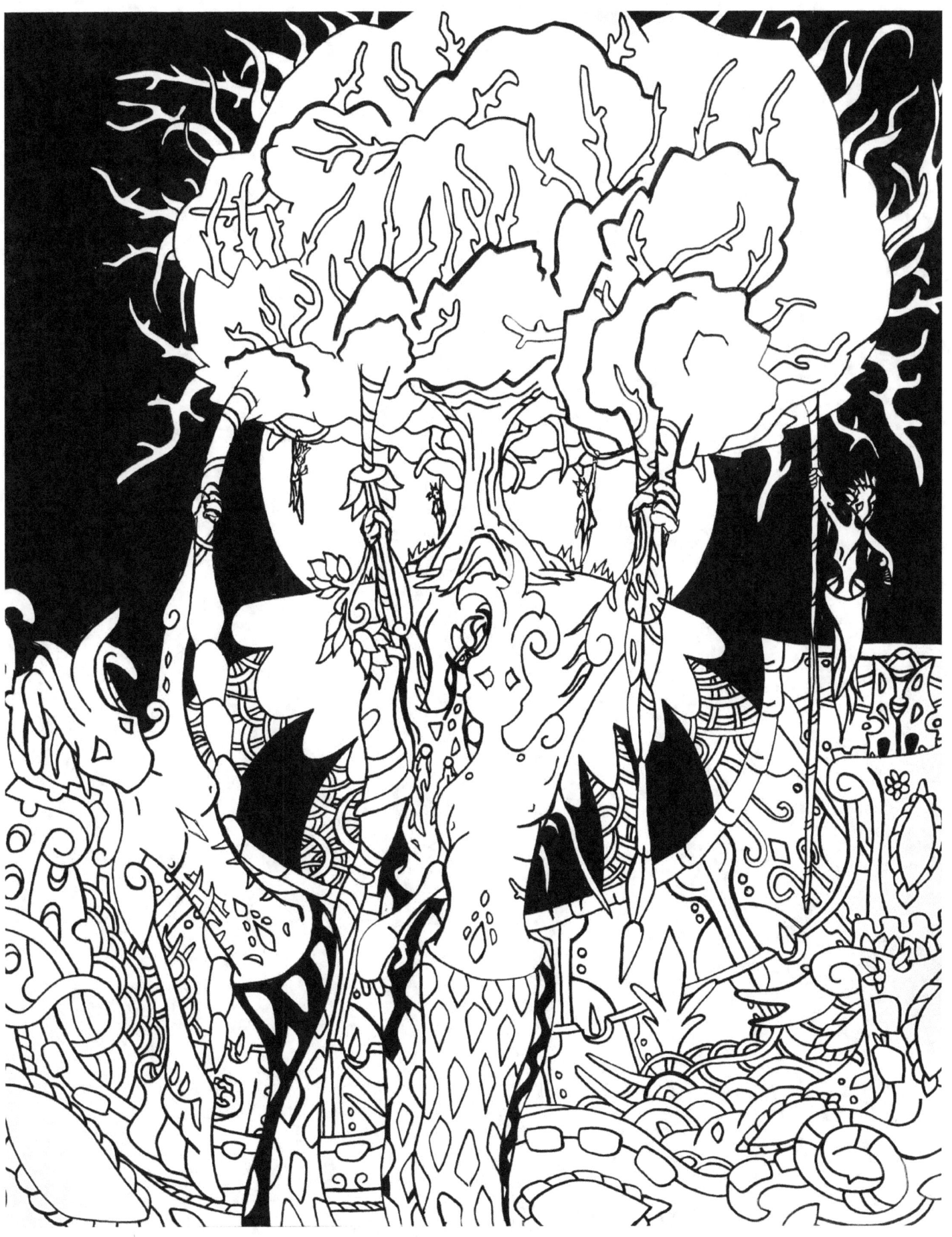

We Walk Without You

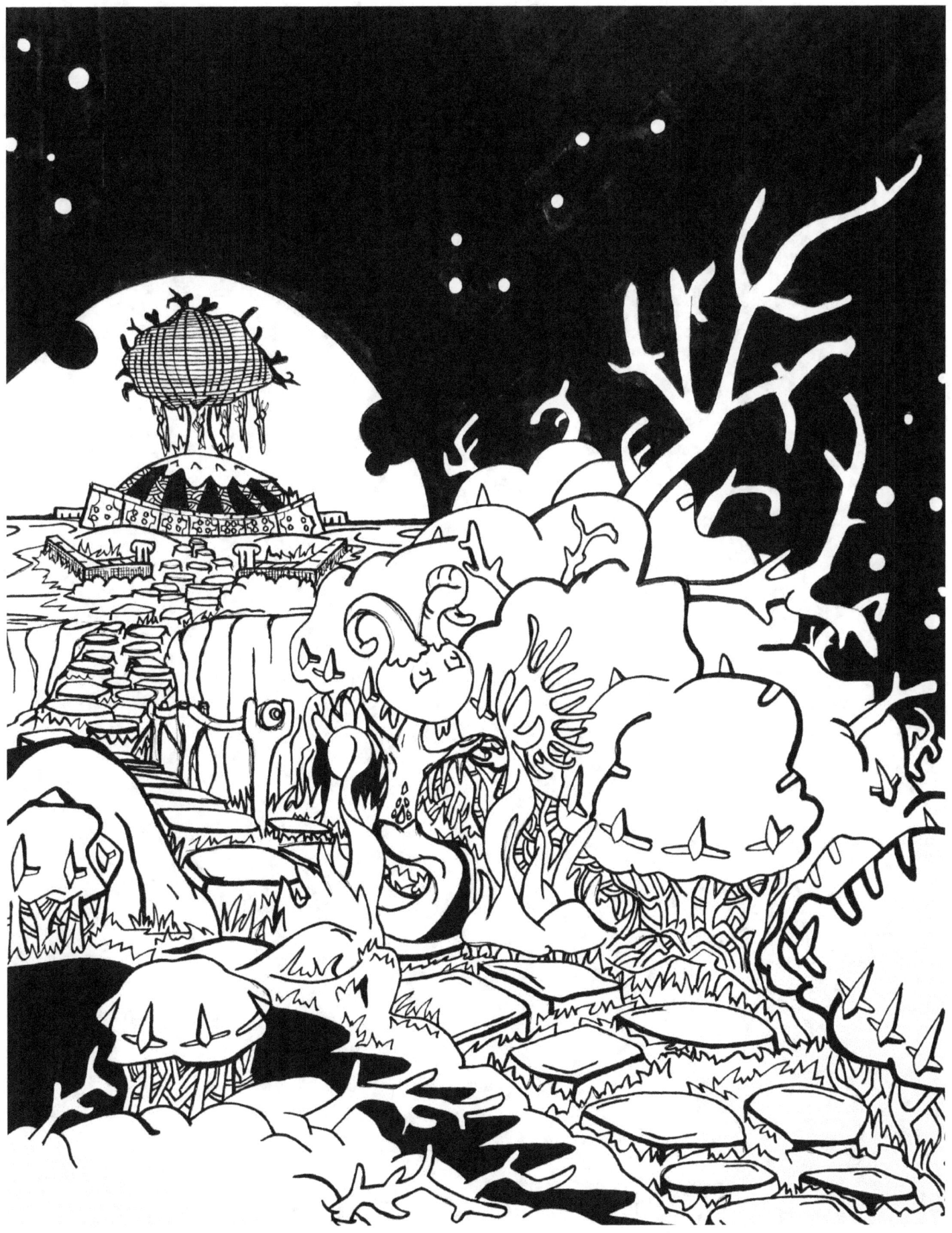

Rest In Peace Eternal

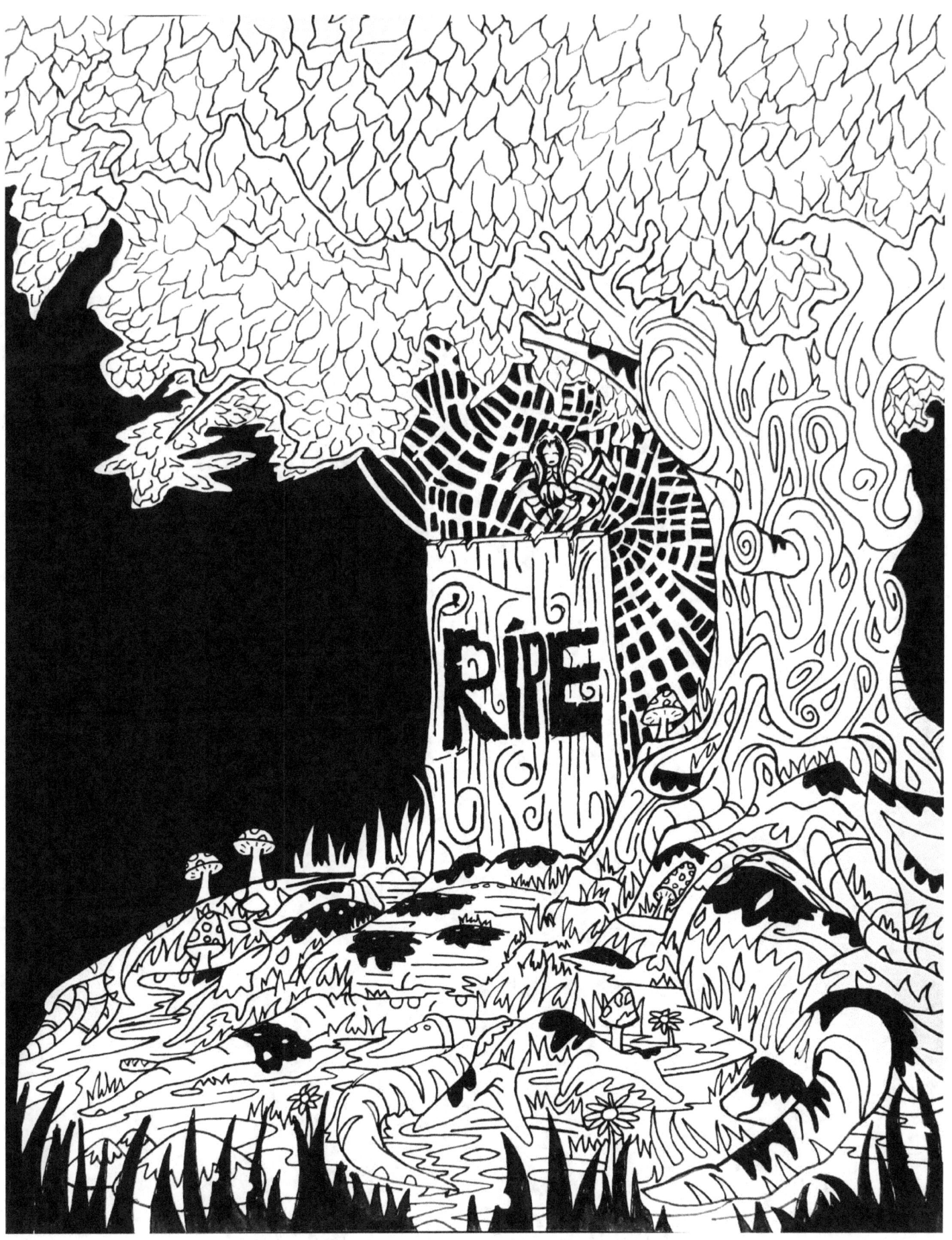

Patience Of Our Beloved

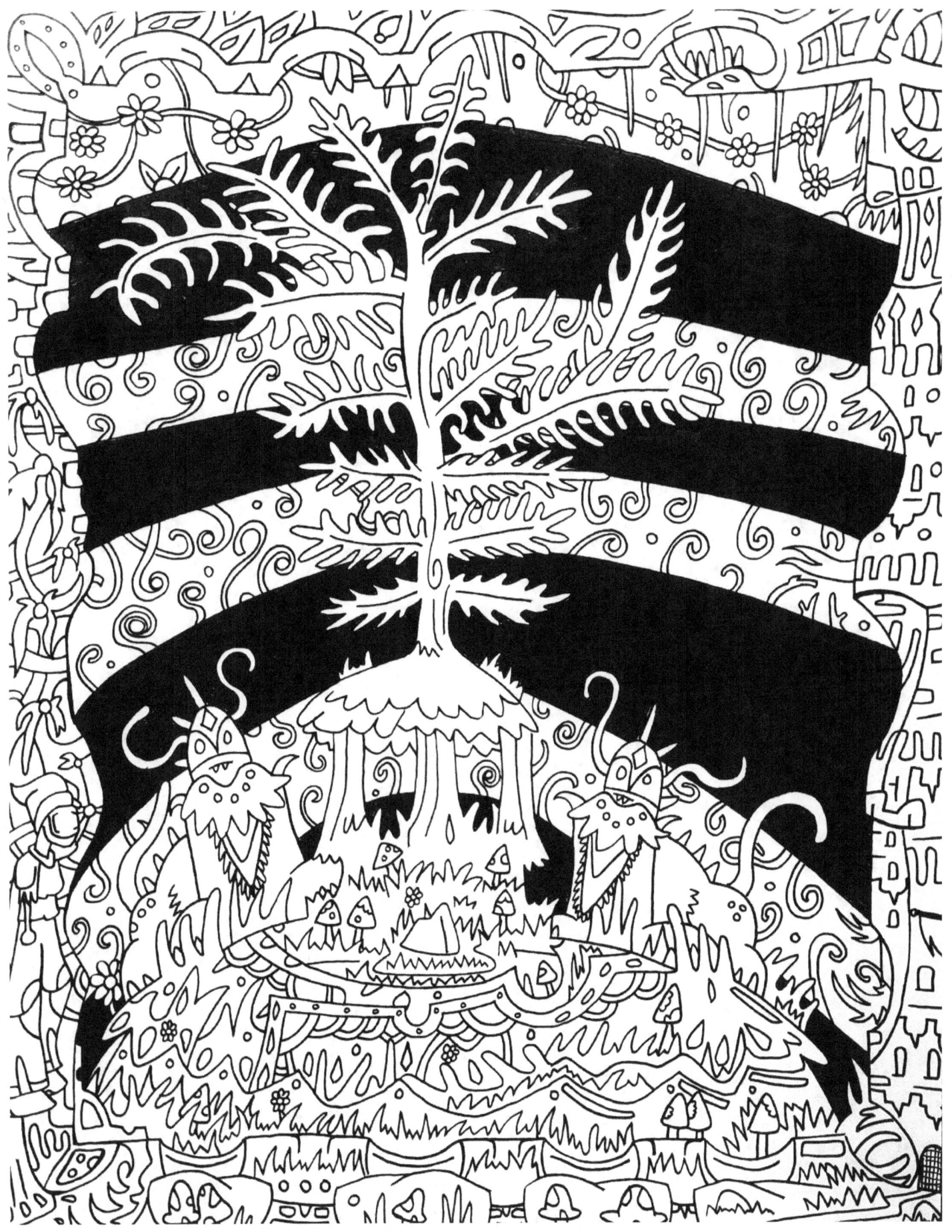

Trusted Instincts

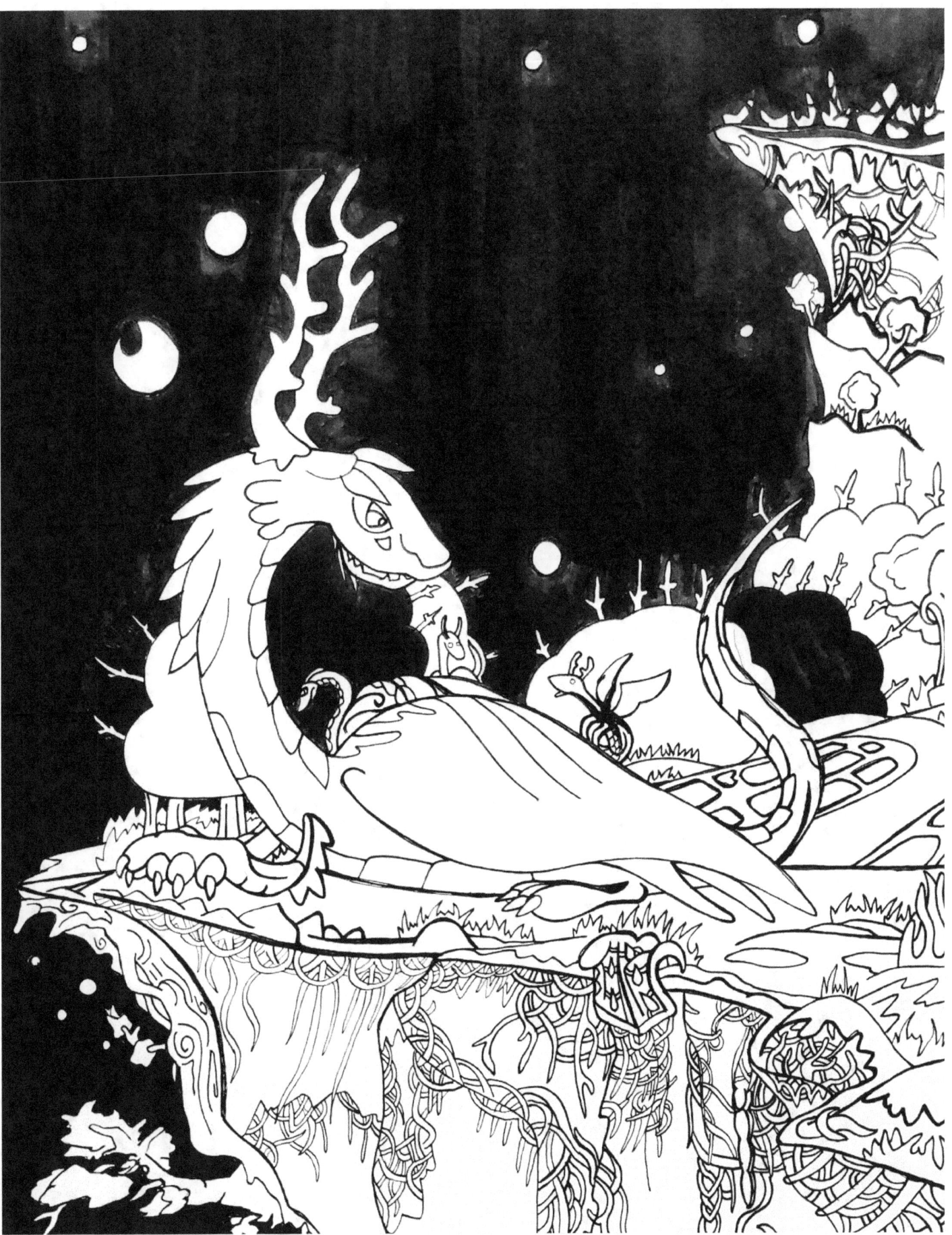

Circle Of Protection

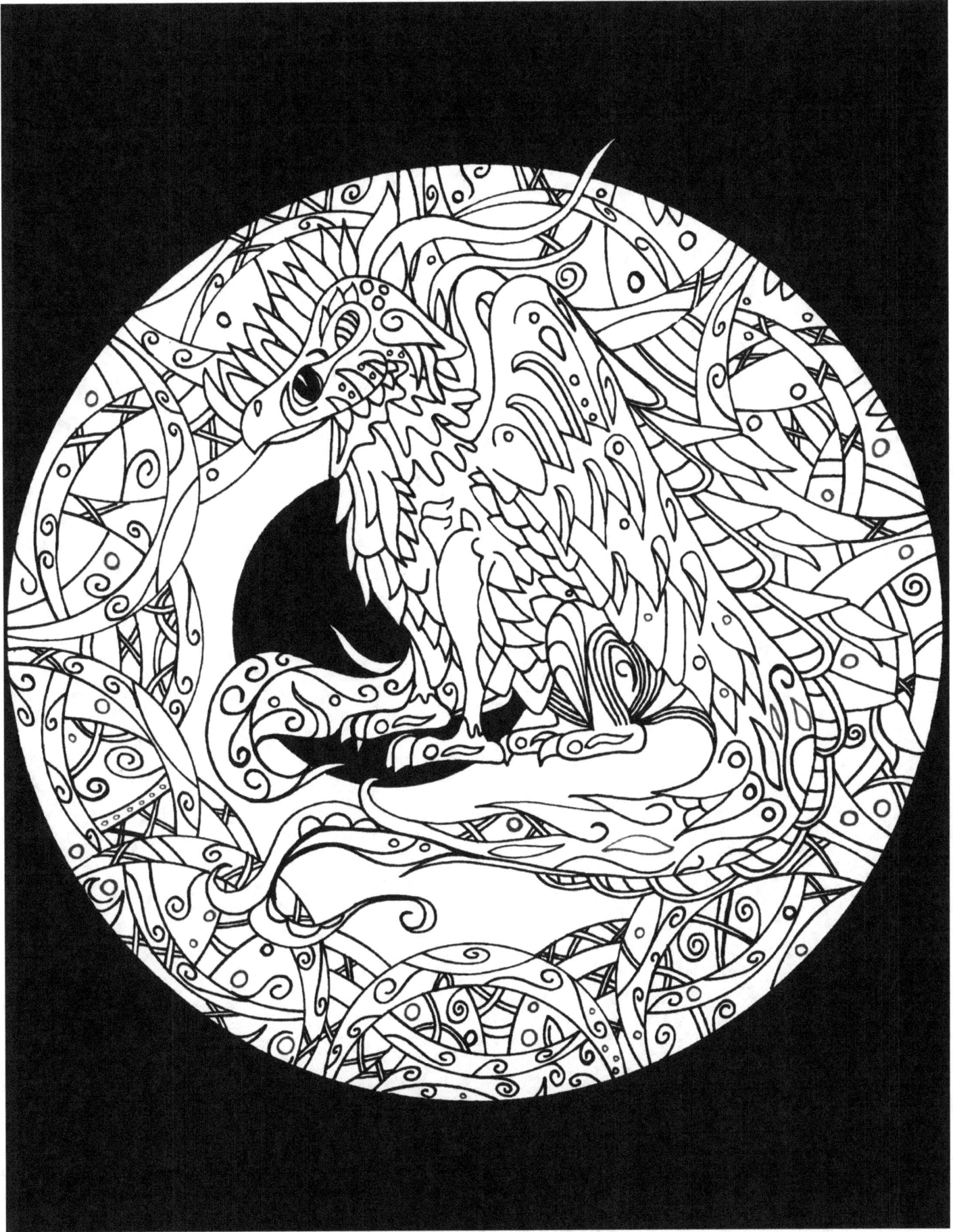

Elusive Spirits

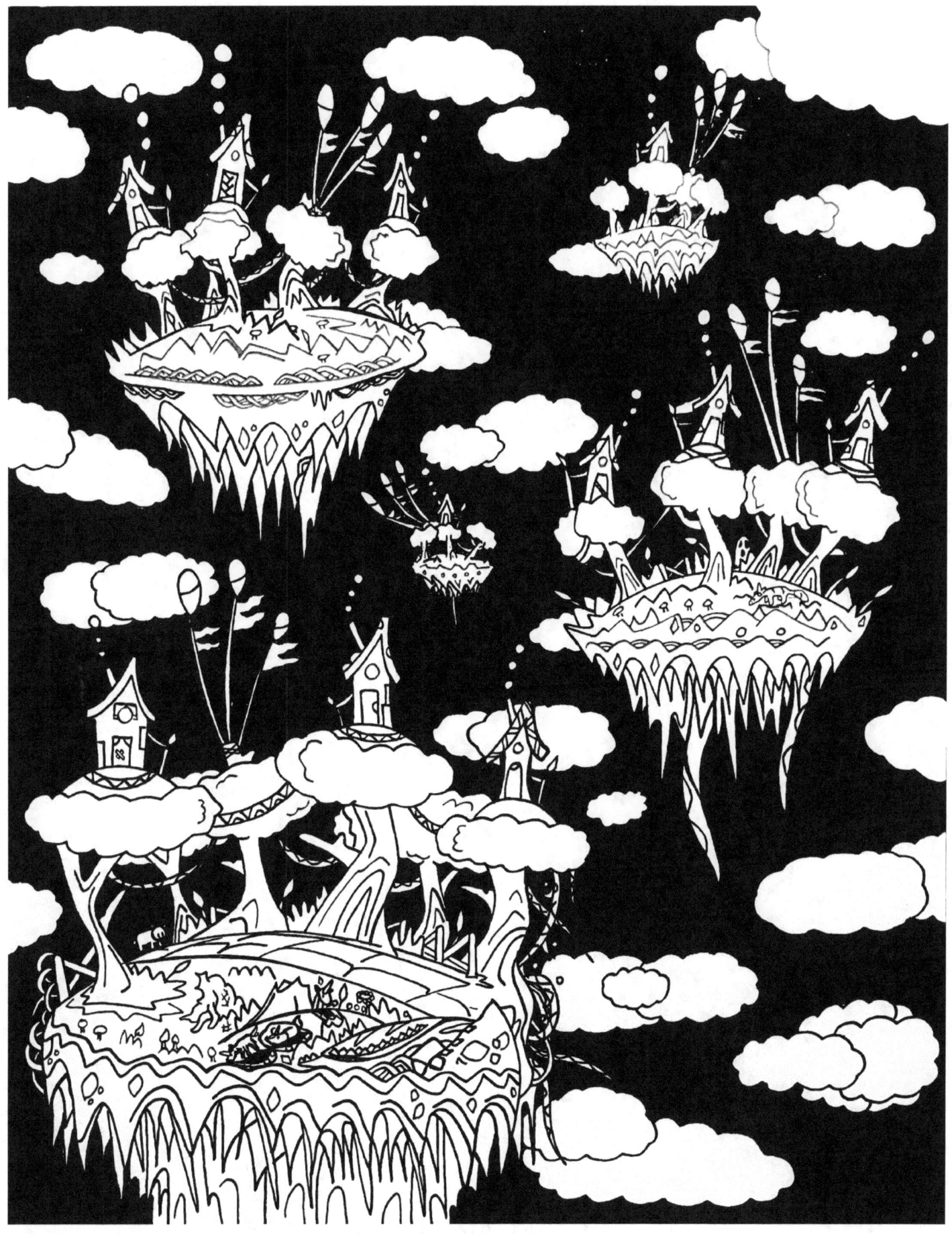

Understanding Balance

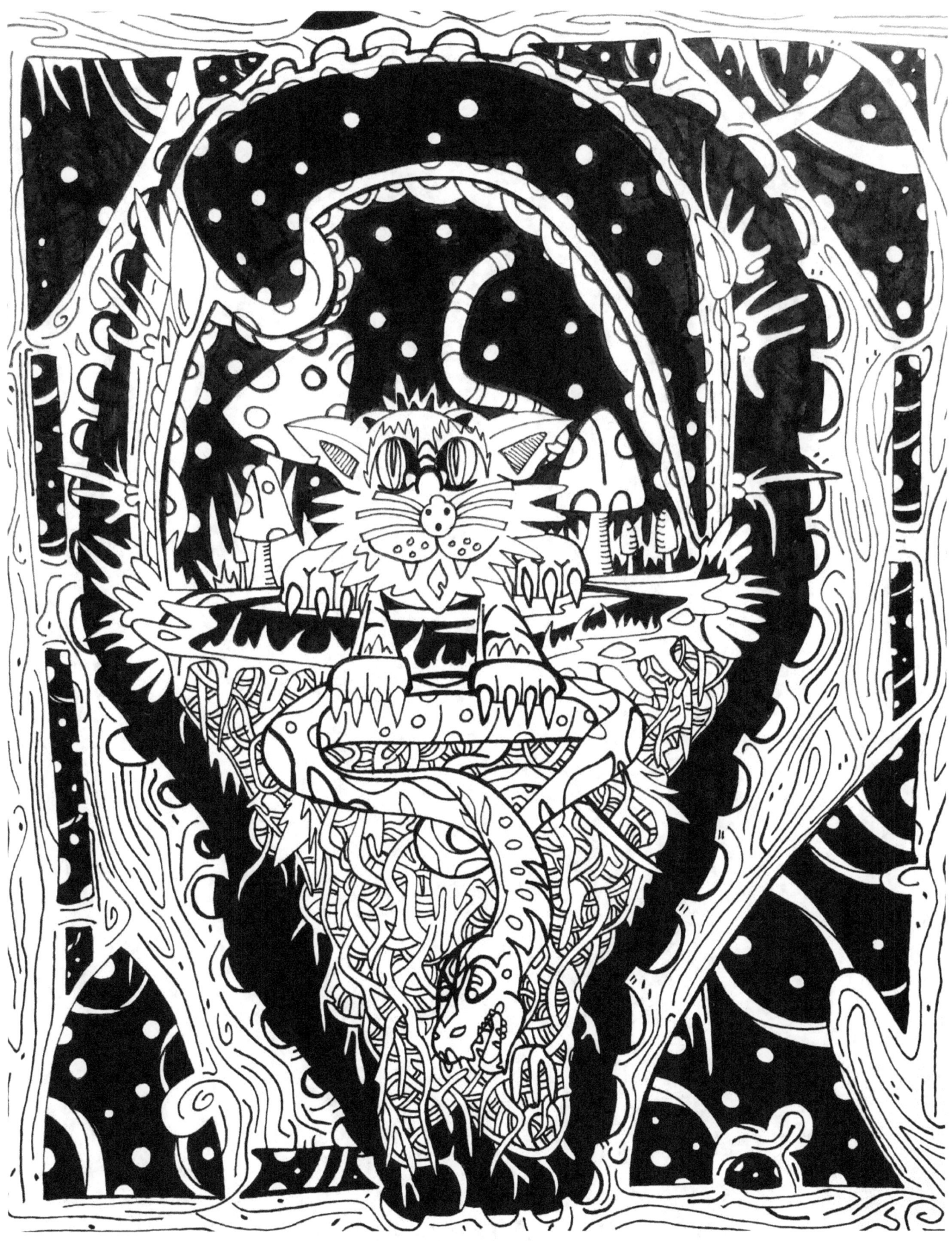

Your World Is Not My World

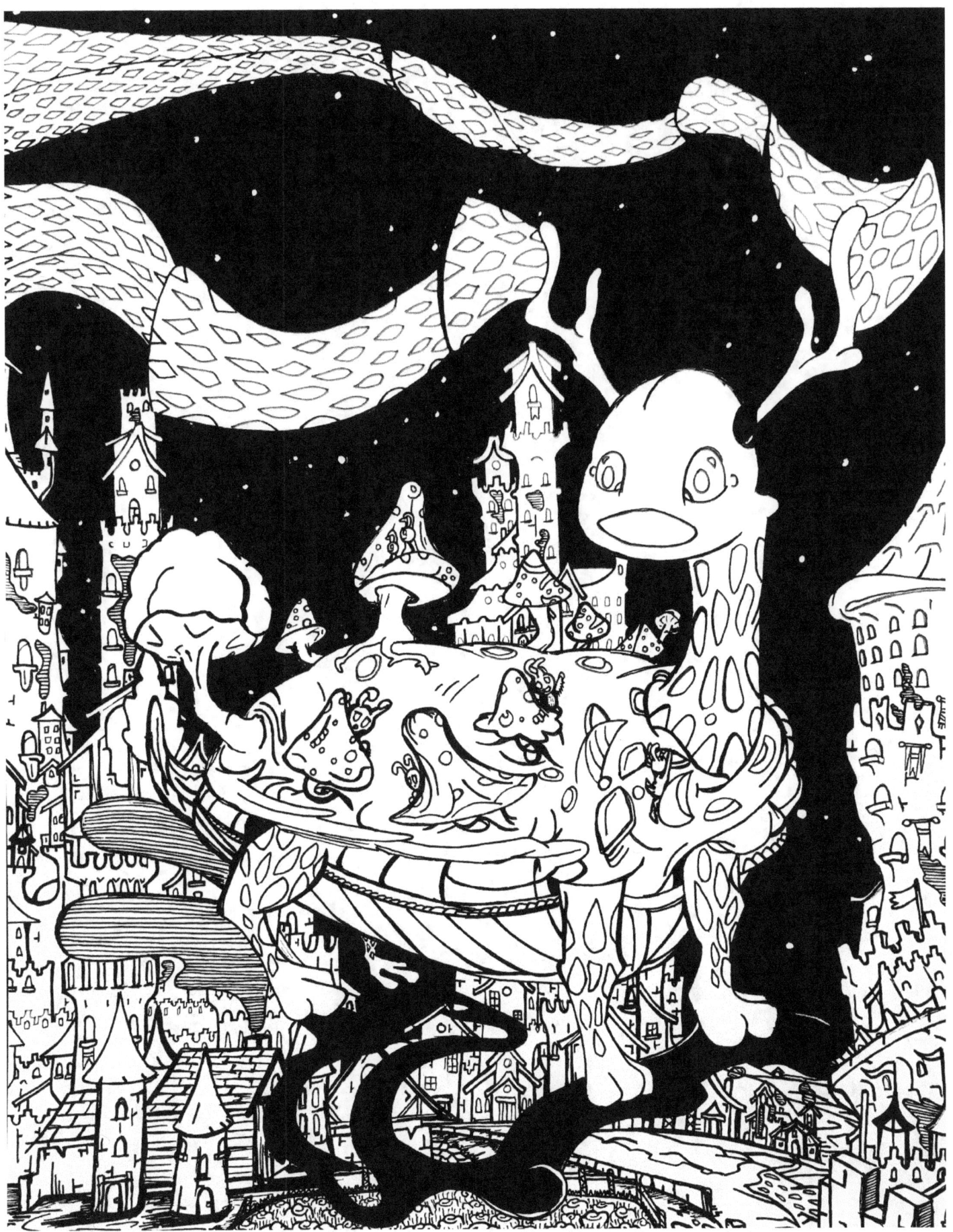

Martyrdom Of The Old Ones

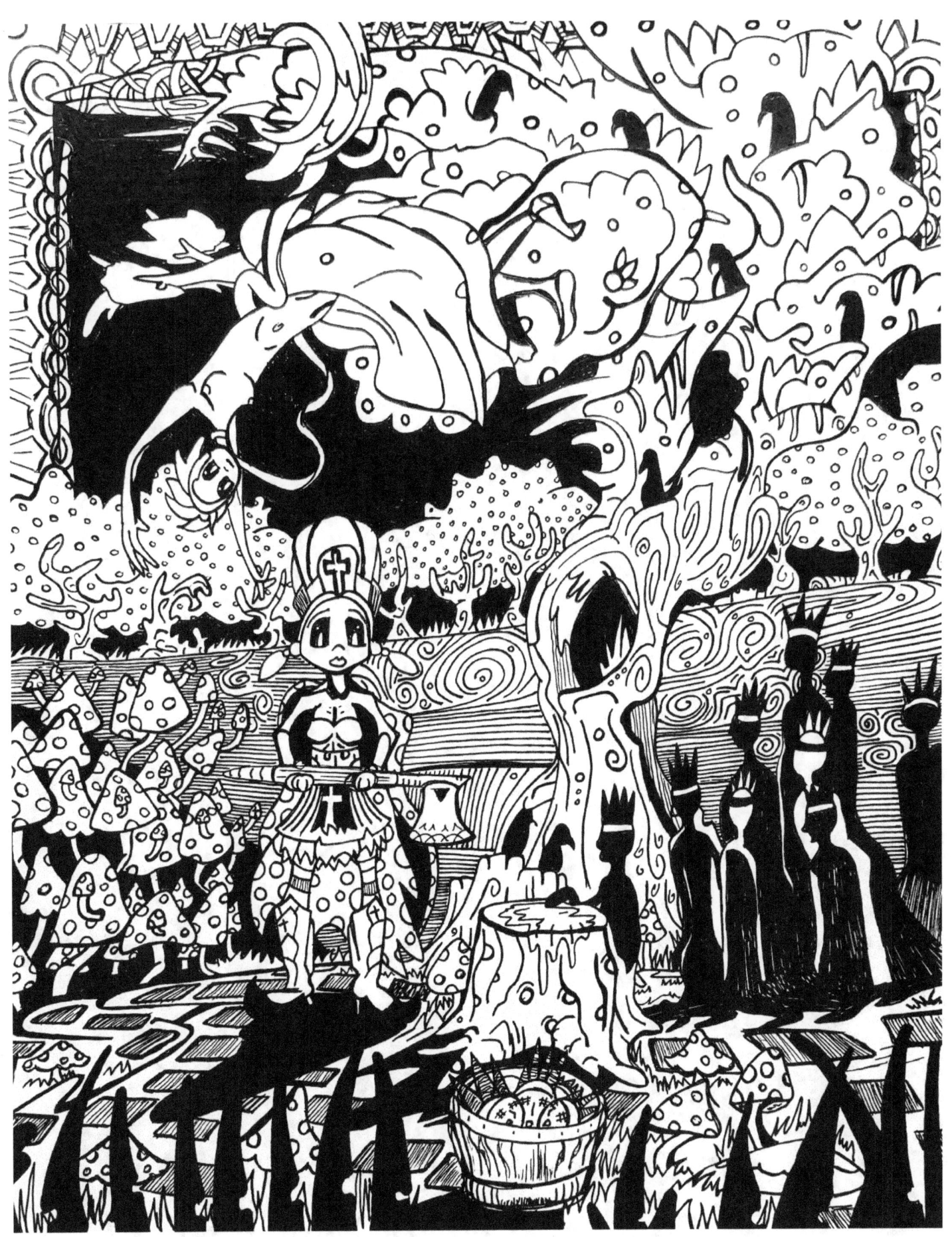

To Return Is To Remember

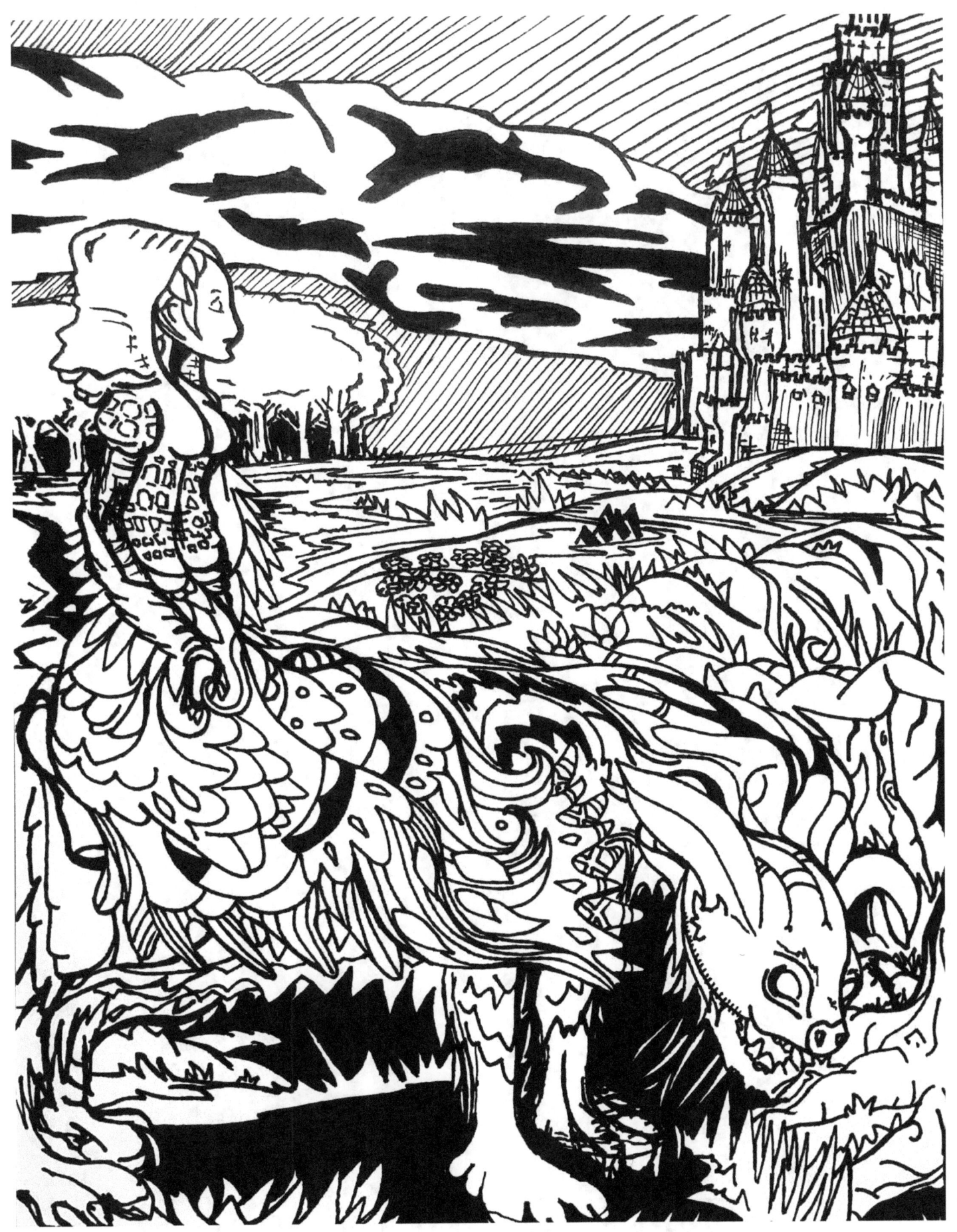

This Is Our Imagination

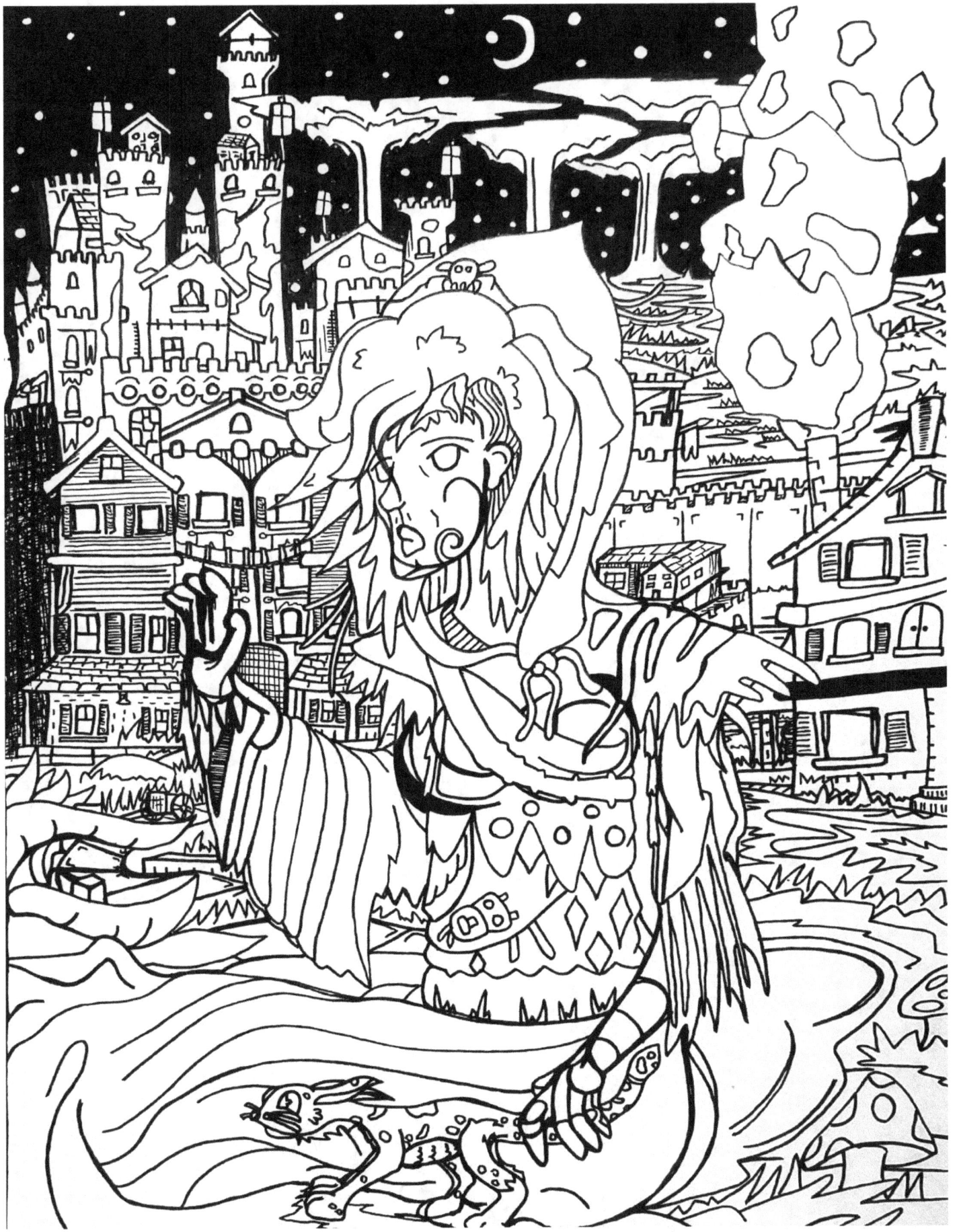

Embrace The End

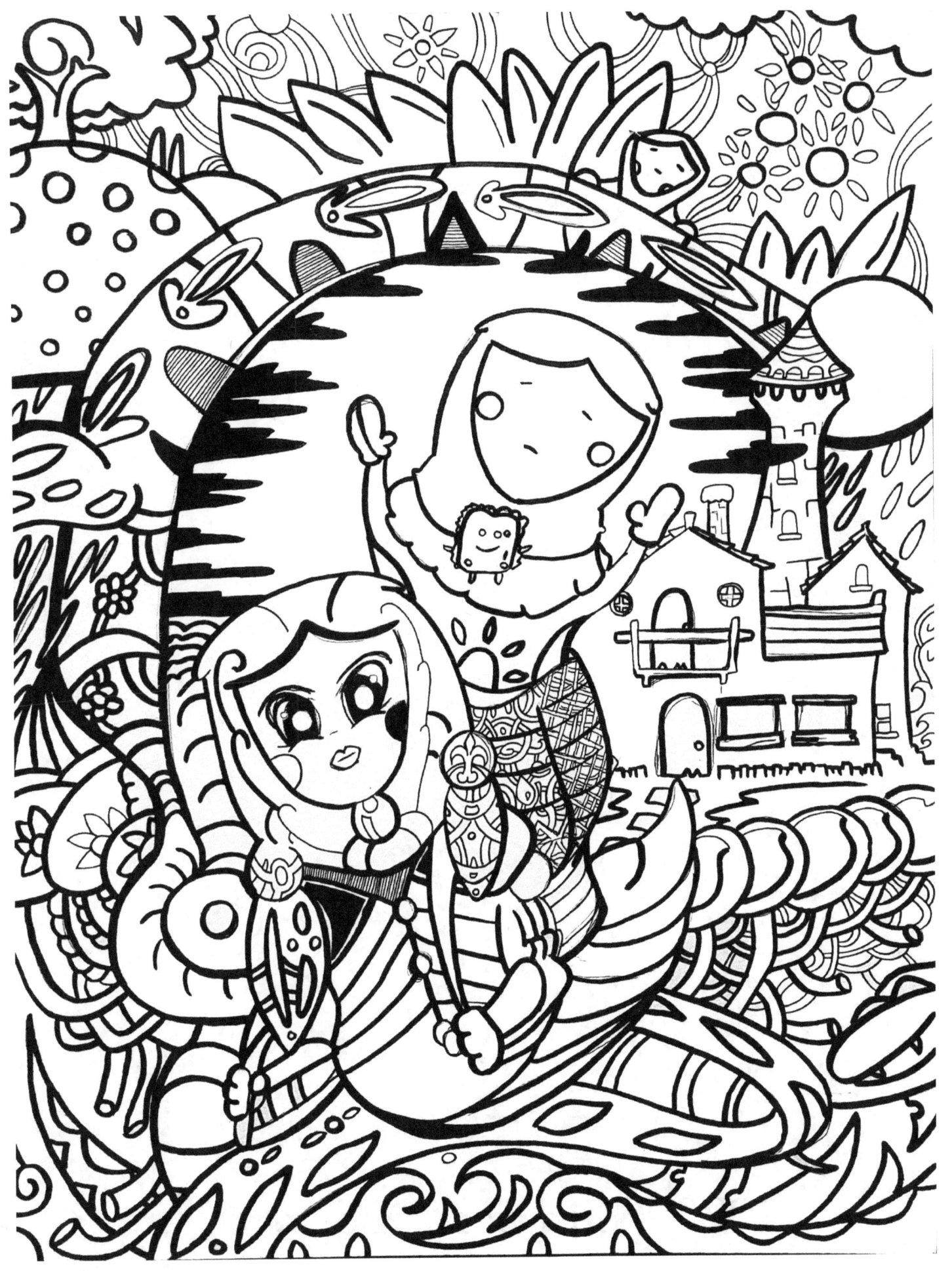

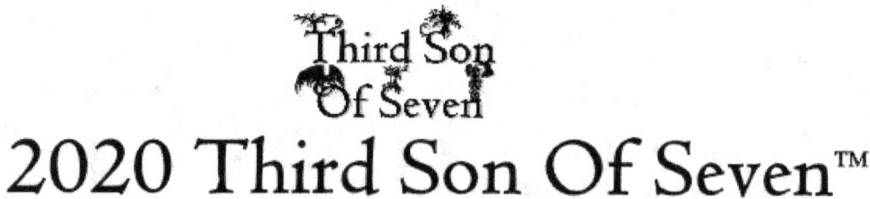

www.ingramcontent.com/pod-product-compliance
Lightning Source LLC
Chambersburg PA
CBHW081059240526
45465CB00025B/2751